Chelmsford
Past & Present

JOHN MARRIAGE

SUTTON PUBLISHING LIMITED

Sutton Publishing Limited
Phoenix Mill · Thrupp · Stroud
Gloucestershire · GL5 2BU

First published 2000

Reprinted in 2003, 2004

Title photograph: Tindal Square, *c.* 1905.

British Library Cataloguing in Publication Data
A catalogue record for this book is available from the
British Library.

ISBN 0-7509-2473-X

Typeset in 10.5/13.5 Photina.
Typesetting and origination by
Sutton Publishing Limited.
Printed and bound in England
by J.H. Haynes & Co. Ltd, Sparkford.

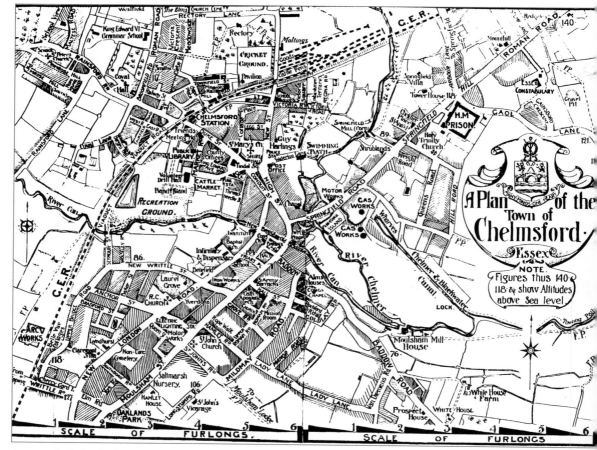

A map of Chelmsford, *c.* 1910.

CONTENTS

An engraving showing the High Street and the newly built Shire Hall, *c.* 1800.

ACKNOWLEDGEMENTS & BIBLIOGRAPHY

The photographs appear by kind permission of the following: Barclays Bank, Mr Boesch, Bolingbroke & Wenley, Essex Record Office, Mr A. Hoy, W. & H. Marriage & Sons Ltd, NatWest Bank, Mrs M. Polley, Mr Shipman, Mrs P. Trevor, Mr R. White. Others come from the author's own collection.

I also acknowledge the help given by my wife, Marion, who cheerfully corrected the grammatical and spelling errors, and made many invaluable suggestions on the content.

Some Essex Water Mills, Hervey Benham (1983)
The Buildings of England: Essex, Nikolaus Pevsner (1954)
The Sleepers and the Shadows, vols 1 & II, Miss Hilda Grieves (Essex Record Office, 1988, 1994)
History, Gazetteer & Directory of the County of Essex, William White (1848)
Chelmsford in Old Photographs, John Marriage (1996)

INTRODUCTION

Chelmsford at the second millennium is a pleasant, modern town within easy commuting distance of the Greater London area and Thameside, where many of its citizens now work. However, it is also a town with a considerable history, although on a brief tour this is not immediately apparent, as many of its older buildings were replaced in the 1960s.

The first recorded settlement in the vicinity was in Roman times, when a small community developed on the south side of the River Can next to the important Roman highway from Colchester to London. It is known to have been large enough to have a substantial temple and a *Mansio*, together with a garrison to guard the road from hostile Celts. Some historians have identified the little town as *Caesarmagus* (Caesar's field). However, it was probably abandoned when the Legions returned to Rome in the fourth century, the Anglo-Saxons invaded eastern England and the Dark Ages descended. Initially, the less cultured invaders had little use for either towns or roads but they later established a market town at Writtle, where King John had a hunting lodge, and the site of *Caesarmagus* was recolonised by a Saxon settler named *Mul*, hence *Mulsham*. During Roman times there had probably been a bridge over both rivers, which collapsed after they left. With its disappearance most travellers bypassed the area, going instead through Writtle to reach Bury St Edmunds and Norwich, thereby avoiding the difficult marshy waste at the junction of the rivers Can and Chelmer at Moulsham.

The history of Chelmsford really began in 1100 when Maurice, Bishop of London, built a bridge over the River Can, at a place called *Ceolmaer's Ford*, thereby restoring the route from London to Norwich to its original Roman alignment and returning the road to its former importance. The construction of the bridge was followed in 1199 when King John granted a charter to the newly installed Bishop William de Sainte-Mere-Eglise, authorising the establishment of a market on a small area of land between the Can and the Chelmer on the site of the present High Street. The Bishop's surveyors laid out a series of extended rectangular plots of regular dimensions around a long wedge-shaped central market area, with each plot running down to the rivers at the rear. Permanent buildings were quickly established facing the market. Writtle, faced by the superior trading position of the new town, rapidly declined in importance, its market evaporated and it soon regressed to a small village.

Fortuitously, the little town was sited almost in the centre of Essex and throughout the medieval period was able to offer services to travellers on the Essex Great Road to and from Colchester, Harwich and Norwich with hotels, hostels, blacksmiths, carriage makers and all the other requirements of travellers. The varied soil in the locality led to the establishment of different forms of agriculture, with Chelmsford the natural trading place for produce. The plentiful supply of river water made it a suitable site for various traditional industries, such as flour milling, brewing and tanneries.

Roads radiating to all parts of the county became established and, despite Chelmsford remaining considerably smaller than the more ancient town of Colchester, its central location in Essex resulted at an early date in county town status, where most local administration was conducted, a role it still retains. In the eighteenth century it was an important stop for scheduled mail and coach services from London to the port of Harwich as well as Norwich, Bury St Edmunds and Sudbury. Many animals were driven through the town 'on the hoof' on their way to the London markets.

In 1797 the town received a further impetus to growth with the construction of the Chelmer & Blackwater Navigation, under the overall direction of John Rennie, the famous eighteenth-century civil engineer. His work enabled cargo barges to travel to and from the Blackwater estuary carrying supplies and materials. Each boat carried a load of some 30 tons and was far more efficient than the heavy cumbersome wagons using the rough roads of the time. Coal became available as a cheap fuel and this led to new industries relying on steam power becoming established in the town. Early the next century the first railways started to be built in Britain. In 1840 the Eastern Counties Railway's line from London was routed through the locality to Colchester and Norwich.

At about the same time land on the south-east side of the town became available for development, as a result of the freeing of the Mildmay entail, and the factories of Hoffmann's (ball-bearing makers), Crompton's (electrical engineers) and Marconi (radio manufacturers) became established in the town, to join a wealth of smaller firms, including Clarkson's, who made steam-powered buses. This firm was later to become the Eastern National Bus Company, still to be seen on our streets. During their peak in the 1940s these firms employed many thousands of workers. Today the town is of far less eminence as an industrial centre, although Marconi has grown to international importance. The former Crompton's factory in Writtle Road is now in process of being redeveloped for housing purposes, whilst the recently created Anglia Polytechnic University has been built on the site previously occupied by Hoffmann's. Nevertheless, the town remains an important administrative centre for both local and national government, including the Essex Police Authority. It also has several National Health and private hospitals and many commercial offices have been established.

Chelmsford received a Royal Charter in 1888 promoting its status to a municipal borough, with Frederick Chancellor, a local architect and businessman, its first mayor. Since then, keeping pace with the growth of the town, the borough boundaries have been extended several times, the latest being in 1974, when the borough was amalgamated with the surrounding rural district into a single administrative unit.

Since the end of the Second World War huge changes have been seen, more drastic and far reaching than any experienced throughout any of the previous centuries. The electrification of the railway, by stages, from Liverpool Street through Chelmsford to Colchester and beyond, with a consequent improvement to passenger services, made the town for the first time attractive to large numbers of commuters. Housing estates sprang up on its perimeter – a process which is still continuing, apparently without pause. Sadly, during the 1960s a complete side of picturesque Tindal Street was bulldozed away and replaced by the dull but efficient High Chelmer shopping precinct, greatly expanding local shopping facilities. At the same time the long-established cattle market was moved away from the centre and the former open-air retail market shoehorned under a new 1,000-space multi-storey car park, strategically sited next to The Parkway, a completely new dual carriageway, which surgically sliced its way through houses and open space from Baddow Road to Rainsford Road. Almost concurrently the River Authority carried out a massive flood prevention scheme, widening and deepening both the River Can and the Chelmer as they passed through the town centre, thereby overcoming the age-old problem of regular winter flooding, which until then had plagued many of the older areas.

Today the central area is pedestrianised and is now one of the largest shopping centres in Essex, rivalling Lakeside at Thurrock in importance and turnover. In recent years many good-quality stores have established branches. Entertainment is provided by two theatres, a multi-screen cinema and many nightclubs. Despite rumours of a possible move, the Essex Cricket Club still plays in the heart of the town and remains a popular venue in the summer, though sadly the former Chelmsford City Football Club ground, sited nearby, is now in progress of being redeveloped. Despite this regrettable loss of open land, Chelmsford still remains fortunate in having a string of well-kept parks and open spaces reaching right to its heart from the open countryside beyond. The historic High Street – which retains its medieval shape – now links High Chelmer with The Meadows, a new and attractive shopping precinct, daringly sited with frontages to both rivers. Some of the older buildings, including St Mary's Cathedral and the striking Shire Hall, survive. The latter, an impressive eighteenth-century building, still dominates the head of High Street, despite all the changes around. In recent times many cafés and restaurants have opened at waterside sites, and with the recent laying of colourful paviors and the introduction of attractive street furniture the centre has a bright and cheerful air, popular with shoppers and pedestrians alike.

1

Town Centre

Children gather in front of the Conduit, at the junction of Springfield Road and High Street, *c.* 1900. It was later moved to the Tower Gardens in Admirals Park and has now been replaced by a colourful town sign on the same spot.

Chelmsford High Street, *c.* 1930. The Shire Hall stands at the top of a shallow incline dominating the wedge-shaped, former market area. In the distance there is a glimpse of the huge Marconi masts, which once provided a local landmark.

Most of the buildings remain from earlier times, although many of the shops have migrated to the nearby precincts. The main physical change has been the elimination of motor vehicles from the highway.

The High Street from the Shire Hall forecourt, *c.* 1900. The buildings facing High Street were mostly of similar dimensions, giving a harmonious appearance. As an important market town it was common for livestock to be driven through the main streets to and from market. In the foreground, in a place of honour, was the *Sebastopol* cannon, presented to the town in 1858 by Major S.J. Skinner, commemorating the Chelmsford Agricultural Society's show in New Street.

The cannon and its plinth were removed to Oaklands Park in the 1930s. High Street was pedestrianised in the 1990s, creating a large traffic-free concourse. However, many of the flanking buildings remain, including Barclays Bank and the Saracens Head Hotel. Fred Spalding's old shop is now occupied by the Abbey National, whilst NatWest, previously installed within an Edwardian building, has expanded into a large 1960s building, which contrasts with the traditional style of the adjacent buildings.

In 1935 the increasing intrusion of the motor car resulted in the installation of traffic islands in High Street. In an attempt at modernisation, several of the original Georgian buildings had been refronted in a more intrusive 1930s commercial style. On the right is the original home of the long-established local weekly newspaper, the *Essex Chronicle*, now at the Widford industrial estate.

The pedestrianisation of High Street in the 1990s created a pleasant open area, flanked by many of the buildings seen in the earlier scene, though their uses have changed. Blocking the view at the bottom of the High Street is the 1960s Cater House, undoubtedly the ugliest building in the town, bar the nearby Market Road multi-storey car park.

From small beginnings Bond's gradually expanded along the north-east side of High Street, taking over adjoining shops and houses, converting them into a single operation and becoming the town's first departmental store. It was eventually sold to Debenham's, the London-based store.

Bond's still occupies the same site, but with very substantial extensions at the rear.

The interior of Barclays Bank, 1950. Although neon lighting had made its appearance, the banking hall was otherwise unchanged from its original Edwardian design, with extensive mahogany counters and eye-level grilles, through which the tellers (all male in those days) conducted the transactions.

In more recent years the banking hall has been completely remodelled, with a much smaller secure area and with the addition of open-plan office stations, each fitted with computer terminals.

Towards the end of the nineteenth century Wenley & Son took over and occupied a three-storey house on the south-western side of High Street. The ground floor was converted into a furniture shop, whilst the family lived above. The building was destroyed by fire in 1947.

The premises were subsequently rebuilt as a departmental shop, amalgamating with Bolingbroke's, also destroyed by fire, who occupied the adjoining building. In April 2000 the shop closed and is yet again in process of redevelopment.

This attractive Victorian terrace built in 1895 occupied the frontage of New London Road between the River Can and Tindal Street. The Chelmsford and Essex Museum originated in the square pillared building seen in the distance, and later moved to the present Anglia Polytechnic University's Chancellor Building, in Victoria Road South, until it finally became established in Oaklands Park, *c.* 1933.

The whole terrace was demolished in the 1960s to make way for a row of new lock-up shops forming part of the efficient, but characterless, High Chelmer shopping precinct.

he success of Wenley &
on's furniture business in
igh Street soon led to the
rm expanding, in about
920 and 1930, into
dditional showrooms and
orage area by utilising the
rmer garden at the rear of
eir property, which
rtuitously had a long
ontage to New London
oad. A covered arcade
onnected New London Road
nd High Street. This was a
opular feature, whose
isappearance after the fire
as long been mourned by
lder Chelmsfordians.

art of Wenley's shop (centre) in New London Road survived the 1947 fire and was incorporated into the new
evelopment. Now, in 2000, the whole site is again the subject of redevelopment.

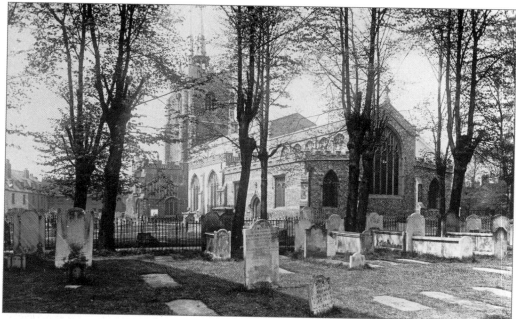

The Anglican Diocese of Chelmsford, which covers the entire geographical county of Essex, was created in 1913. St Mary's, previously the parish church of Chelmsford, was then raised to the status of cathedral. Although partly obscured by the Shire Hall, its dominant feature when seen from afar is the fifteenth-century buttressed west tower with its decorated battlements. The tower is surmounted by a leaded needle spire. It is pictured here prior to enlargements in the 1930s.

Entering the new millennium, the Cathedral has changed little outwardly, even though considerable alterations have taken place inside. The iron railings marking the line of footpaths through the graveyard were swept away during the war and more recently many of the old headstones have been removed, creating a manicured lawn aspect.

The interior of St Mary's Cathedral, showing the fifteenth-century nave piers and the ribbed, coved Tudor-style ceiling, installed in 1899 after the famous Essex earthquake that year damaged the building.

In the 1980s the interior of the church was remodelled when the Victorian pews were removed. In recent years, in addition to its normal duties, the Cathedral has become an important venue for cultural activities, such as music festivals.

Tindal Square was an important meeting area for townspeople, ranging from the weekly market to celebrations of national and local events. Here, in about 1905, standing behind the statue of Judge Tindal, is the Corn Exchange, built in 1857 to a neo-Renaissance style, from a design by Frederick Chancellor. Although intended primarily for agricultural purposes, until its sad demolition in the 1960s it was extensively used for public activities as diverse as dog shows, wrestling and dancing. The square is named after Sir Nicholas Tindal, who was born at Coval Hall in 1776 and was educated at Chelmsford Grammar School. During the nineteenth century he became Lord Chief Justice of the Court of Common Pleas.

The square was remodelled in the 1960s and many of the surrounding buildings were replaced. Behind the statue is the entrance to the High Chelmer shopping precinct. The stone-faced building in the distance is a recent extension to County Hall. Traffic has been realigned to pass along Tindal Street, instead of High Street, with the result that the Square is now little more than an awkward traffic junction.

Tindal Square, from Tindal Street, looking towards the Cathedral, *c.* 1945. Fred Spalding, Chelmsford's well-known photographer (many of whose pictures appear in this book), had his studio within the greenhouse-like structure on the roof of the three-storey building to the right of the picture, until he moved in 1895 into premises next to the Saracens Head Hotel.

The buildings on the north side of the square still remain. However, the Corn Exchange, seen on the left of the upper picture, has been superseded by a brick-clad three-storey shop on a new alignment to Tindal Street.

Tindal Square and High Street from Market Road, *c.* 1905, with Judge Tindal's statue impassively watching the passers-by. Adjoining the substantial four-storey Barclays Bank building, is the three-storey eighteenth-century Saracens Head Hotel, formerly one of the town's busiest coaching inns. During the Second World War it was used as a leave centre for members of the USAAF. The attractive buildings on the right of the picture were replaced by two rival bank chambers in 1921.

Modern traffic requirements have resulted in the creation of dedicated vehicle lanes through the square and the upper part of High Street, and large pedestrian areas have been created. In recent years the two bank chambers on the right have been converted into a single local branch, though the individual ornamental classical-style exteriors have not been changed.

For many years the family firm of H. & T.C. Godfrey occupied the premises in Tindal Square vacated by Fred Spalding, and specialised in the sale and hire of sacks and tents, as well as a range of hardware. Their factory was in Moulsham Street. The business closed in about 1985.

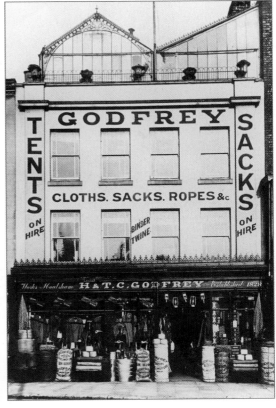

Estate agents are now in the premises: the shop front has been modernised and the sash windows at first-floor level replaced. The building now presents a much blander appearance after the removal of the various advertising signs.

Tindal Street, seen here in about 1905, was undoubtedly the town's most attractive street, containing many interesting old buildings dating back to medieval times. Immediately on the right is the Bell Hotel, demolished by the Council in 1945 as it was derelict and considered unsafe. For a number of years its site housed the town's weekly stall market.

In the 1960s the whole of one side of the street was demolished to make way for the present High Chelmer shopping precinct. The loss of the attractive old buildings has long been regretted by many Chelmsfordians.

The High Street from its junction with New London Road, decorated for Queen Elizabeth's Coronation in 1953. Then, as now, the stone-faced Shire Hall dominated the funnel-shaped area, then open for two-way traffic.

In the late 1990s the road was pedestrianised, with traffic diverted down Tindal Street and the surface relaid with coloured paviors. This has greatly improved the appearance of the historic heart of the town.

These ancient timber-framed buildings, seen here in about 1900, were sited at the junction of New London Road and High Street, and were demolished in the late 1950s to make way for junction improvements. The tall brick structure at the rear was purpose-built for the Norwich Union at the turn of the nineteenth century.

In the late 1950s the site was redeveloped, and a three-storey 'neo-Georgian' building, with shops on the ground floor and offices above, replaced the old cottages.

A view of the lower end of Tindal Street in the early 1960s just prior to its demolition, to make way for the shopping precinct. Wainwright's Milk Bar, on the left, was a Mecca for many young people, including the author and his friends. Nearby was Cramphorn's shop, which had the last Georgian bay window in the town.

The main entrance to the High Chelmer shopping precinct replaces Wainwright's little shop. The present featureless brick wall of the precinct alongside Tindal Street has, unfortunately, massively changed the appearance of this once picturesque street.

The Bell Hotel was an attractive old timber-framed building which closed at the outbreak of the Second World War, never to reopen. However, it had a brief moment of glory when part was used as committee rooms for the successful parliamentary candidate during a wartime by-election, caused by the death, in action, of the standing MP. It was pulled down a short time afterwards as it had become unsafe.

This single-storey brick precinct building was built on the frontage of Tindal Street on approximately the same spot.

One of the historic features of the town was the existence of long narrow yards, leading at right angles away from High Street and Tindal Street, providing stabling, storage accommodation and, in some cases, access to houses. One such yard was provided by the Bell Hotel with its entrance from Tindal Street, via a tunnel under the building.

As a result of redevelopment throughout the town centre, only two of these yards – both in High Street – still exist. Bell Yard is now part of a large service area for the High Chelmer shopping precinct.

High Street towards the Shire Hall, *c.* 1945. On the right is Bond's, then Chelmsford's only departmental store. Its slogan, 'You can get it at Bond's', was known all over mid-Essex, being prominently displayed on many of the buses. The four-storey island building on the left was occupied by Clarke's, still one of Chelmsford's leading stationers and booksellers.

With the banning of vehicular traffic in part of the town centre pedestrians have regained the freedom to wander along the High Street, which, with the introduction of tree planting, has acquired a softer, more welcoming appearance. Lloyds TSB now occupy the entire island site, whilst Clarke's have a shop in High Chelmer.

High Street, towards Springfield Road, with the long façade of Bond's, on the left, *c.* 1945. On the right are Wenley's and Bolingbroke's, then two separate shops. Both premises were still in their wartime mode, with most of their window area covered with protective plywood and only a small area of glass exposed.

In the 1990s the High Street was pedestrianised and landscaped. The former Bond's store has been acquired by Debenham's and expanded, whilst both Wenley's and Bolingbroke's, and most of the other adjoining buildings have been rebuilt.

The junction of High Street with Springfield Road, *c.* 1930. High Street was then part of the main road to and from East Anglia, busy with traffic waiting to turn right towards Colchester. The elegant Conduit, in earlier times installed as an attractive piece of street furniture, had become a mere traffic island, festooned with road signs. It was removed to Admirals Park several years later.

During the last years of the twentieth century High Street was reclaimed by pedestrians, and the junction has since became a meeting place for Chelmsfordians and a venue for street events. A new sign, incorporating the town's coat of arms, stands where the old Conduit used to be.

Capital & Counties built this classical-style four-storey building in 1905, on part of the island site at the junction of New London Road and High Street. The remainder of the area was occupied by another four-storey building which had shops on the ground floor and residential accommodation over. It was later rebuilt by Clarke's stationers and booksellers, who remained there until the 1960s when they moved to High Chelmer.

The entire island site is now occupied by Lloyds TSB, a successor bank to Capital & Counties.

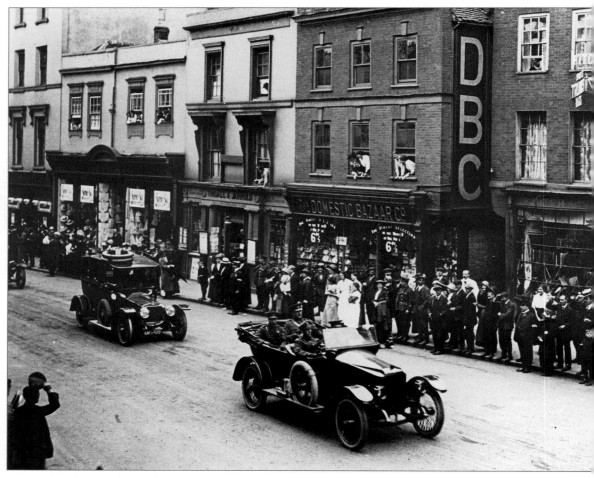

King George V making his only visit to Chelmsford, 14 October 1914, in an open-top Vauxhall, watched by some of his loyal subjects. Unlike today, when elaborate precautions must be taken, his security was minimal and there is little sign of any police or security presence. His Majesty later inspected Territorials of the South Midland Division, who paraded in Hylands Park.

Today High Street is normally clear of motor transport except during ceremonial events, but it remains a focal point for Chelmsfordians.

In the early part of the last century the largest stationer and bookseller in the town was Edward Durrant & Co., who occupied a three-storey property in High Street. Like so many other retailers he lived over the premises. Later the site was occupied by a branch of Sainsbury's, who rebuilt the property to their standard design with Georgian-styled upper floors.

Following the 1960s construction of High Chelmer, trade at the upper end of High Street began to decline, and many shops were converted into offices and other commercial premises.

This attractive three-storey property in the High Street was built by the London & County Banking Company in 1905. It consisted of a small banking chamber on the ground floor and living accommodation for the manager on the upper floors. The company was eventually taken over by Westminster Bank.

In the 1960s Westminster Bank combined with the National Provincial Bank, and, on purchasing the adjacent shop, constructed the present ugly and over-dominant NatWest structure, comprising a banking parlour, shops and offices.

Every Friday until the beginning of the last century a well-supported poultry and secondhand market was held in Market Road opposite the livestock pens.

Since the 1960s the entire area has been redeveloped. On the left is the 1990s extension to County Hall, whilst a multi-storey car park (right) has replaced the former livestock pens. Further away, the three-storey building with the logo 'High Chelmer' occupies the site of the town's first fire station.

Chelmsford's Friday market has always been very popular for those seeking a bargain. Once held in High Street, it was transferred in about 1900 to land at the corner of Threadneedle Street and Market Road.

Public conveniences now occupy the latter site. Behind is the multi-storey County Hall, built in stages from the 1930s. The central atrium, linking the two wings, marks the alignment of the former King Edward Avenue, now built over. The still thriving market's present home is under the multi-storey car park in Market Road.

The 1960s brought many changes to the centre of the town. The most dramatic was the construction of the present High Chelmer shopping precinct, which swept away a huge swathe of centuries-old development. This picture shows West Square in about 1970, laid out to a formal rectangular pattern of raised brick-edged gardens with a line of young trees.

Now, after some thirty years, the square has matured, with some of the original saplings growing into respectable trees. The fussy rectangular planting boxes have disappeared and the square has become a popular sitting area.

The main shopping mall of High Chelmer, soon after it was built in the 1960s. For the first time it provided enclosed parades of multiple stores, albeit in a rather dull fashion. It quickly captured a large proportion of the local trade, causing financial problems to many of the long-established traders in High Street, some of whom were able to relocate to the precinct.

Facing competition from the newer Meadows shopping area, the precinct has been completely refurbished and now presents a less clinical appearance.

From 1852 for nearly ninety years this small domed structure, an attractive rotunda known to all as The Conduit, with four Tuscan columns, dominated the junction of Springfield Road and High Street. It was designed at the turn of the nineteenth century and was moved there from Tindal Square. On the left of this picture, *c.* 1900, is the King's Head pub, which has given its name to the present car park. In the distance is the Methodist church.

Time has swept away all the earlier buildings on the left side of the High Street and a branch of Woolworths now occupies the site of the King's Head pub. The massive concrete bulk of Cater House has replaced the church. The Conduit now stands in Admirals Park.

Moulsham Street busy with shoppers and pedestrians, *c.* 1935. The corner shop occupied by Lovedays, the jeweller, marks the entrance to Baddow Road, then the main road to Southend and Maldon. Diagonally opposite stands the Chelmsford Star Co-operative Society's main retail premises, and on the other side of Barrack Street can be spied the white-rendered Bond's furniture store. The latter closed in the 1960s when the firm was taken over by Debenham's.

Moulsham Street in spring 2000 has a more relaxed appearance, with most of the buildings shown in the earlier scene surviving. However, shopfronts have been replaced as occupancy has changed and the Co-operative premises have been completely rebuilt.

Moulsham Street, *c.* 1900. In the distance is the curved balustrade of Moulsham Bridge, with the red-brick former Methodist church behind. On the right is the ornate exterior of the Regent theatre, built on the site of the Cross Keys pub demolished in 1913. When talking pictures swept the country theatres went into sharp decline: the Regent was no exception and converted to a cinema, although shows continued to be staged particularly at Christmas.

Within the last few years the street has been pedestrianised and walkers now have total freedom to stroll its length. After a period as a bingo club the Regent has become a nightclub. Beyond the bridge is the massive concrete-faced bulk of Cater House, an unfortunate legacy of the 1960s. The church was demolished to make room.

Another view of Moulsham Street, *c.* 1912, just prior to the demolition of the Cross Keys and its replacement by the Regent theatre. Nearest the camera is the old-established Hawkes' confectionery shop, which had a factory in New Street, on land now occupied by the police station.

Moulsham Street is now part of an attractive Conservation Area. Rankin's old premises and Hawkes' old shop remain in retail use.

The annual Chelmsford Carnival Procession was a well-established local charitable activity, with the parade passing through the main streets. Like many other sports clubs, the Chelmsford Boating (now Canoe) Club actively supported the event. Here, their entry in about 1955, passing along Moulsham Street, was very simple – a racing kayak mounted on a member's Ford Prefect.

Vehicles are now banned from the street and new tenants now occupy the shops. A hairdresser has replaced the gentlemen's outfitters, whilst the grocer's shop has been converted into part of the extended Co-operative premises.

This typically 1920s three-storey red-brick building at the junction of Moulsham Street with The Friars had lock-up shops on the ground floor with flats above, and replaced several timber-framed medieval buildings, which had formerly stood on the same site.

In the 1960s The Parkway was built along the same alignment, and the building shown above was demolished to make way for the widened carriageway. In 2000 the adjoining building was undergoing repairs.

The Friars, July 1888, from its junction with New London Road during a freak summer flood caused by an extreme thunderstorm, after a period of heavy rain. The road was flooded to a depth of about 2 ft through which pedestrians and traffic had to pass. Until the construction of a massive flood prevention scheme in the 1960s winter floods were an almost annual occurrence. The tall building on the left is The Friars School, used until the late 1930s and demolished after the Second World War.

The Parkway now runs along the same alignment as The Friars, and all the properties seen in the previous picture (above) have been demolished.

This engraving shows the former Chelmsford Gaol, which existed in Moulsham Street beside the Stone Bridge until 1848. It was replaced by the present gaol in Springfield Road, and for a time the site was occupied by a militia barracks and a parade ground. After the soldiers left shops were built fronting Moulsham Street.

Today the brick and slate Victorian terrace remains much the same in appearance, although altered and extended at the rear.

Moulsham Bridge, the town's main crossing of the River Can, *c.* 1905. This single-span bridge was designed by John Johnson in 1787, whilst he was surveyor to the county. The sturdy balusters are made from Coade stone, an artificial material whose formula is now lost. Behind is the Methodist church, built in 1898 on the site of a former public house. On two levels, it had room for 500 worshippers, with a Sunday School at the rear.

The handsome bridge – now for pedestrians only – still remains amid major changes in the immediate locality. The Cater building has replaced the church and a riverside path has been created. There is a glimpse of The Meadows shopping centre on the left.

Moulsham Bridge, from downstream, *c.* 1910. The foliage from a tree growing in a riverside garden frames the scene. On the far side of the river was the red-brick Victorian gothic Methodist church.

In the 1960s the church was replaced by Cater House, creating a real blot on the landscape. A Wimpy bar occupies the ground floor, whilst a radio station and offices are above.

Moulsham Bridge, *c. 1950*. This once carried all the traffic passing through the town to and from London and the coast and, surprisingly, when river works were carried out in the 1960s, was found to have little or no foundations. The lower part of High Street is on the far side of the bridge.

This scene has changed considerably over the last fifty years and the only building common to both pictures is the 1930s Woolworths store, in the distance. The striking gable-ended structure, middle distance, is the entrance to The Meadows shopping precinct.

The former Central Stores of the Chelmsford Star Co-operative Society was at the corner of Barrack Street and Moulsham Street. It was built in 1880 on part of the site of the County Gaol and Militia Parade Ground, with shops at ground floor and basement level, and assembly rooms on the first floor.

The current building replaced the earlier structures in the 1970s. It shadows its original form and scale, providing a pleasing feature in this part of the town centre. It is in use as part of the Co-operative's main store.

Baddow Road near its junction with Moulsham Street, awash with water in 1888 during the notorious summer flood, recorded on camera by Fred Spalding.

The 1960s flood prevention scheme has made the properties secure from all but the most exceptional wet weather, and the main problem now is saturation of the street by parked cars.

The Ritz in Baddow Road was the most luxurious and modern cinema in the town when built in the 1930s by Eastern Counties Cinemas. It included a large auditorium, a balcony and a dance hall over the foyer. It was subsequently renamed and taken over by the Odeon group, and was demolished in the 1970s.

The land is now occupied by a brick-faced multi-storey car park of striking appearance, and a new multi-screen Odeon cinema has been built nearby.

At the turn of the twentieth century Munnion & Sons, Coachbuilders, occupied these premises in Springfield Road, next to the River Chelmer. Coachwork for Clarkson's steam buses was fabricated here, as well as bodywork for Bentall motor cars. Later in the century the buildings were occupied as a dairy and more recently as shops.

The site now forms part of The Meadows shopping precinct; the replacement building curiously echoes the earlier structure in size and shape.

The River Can from Moulsham Bridge, *c.* 1935. On the left, part of the Congregational church can be glimpsed. It was demolished in the 1960s to make way for an extension to the Co-operative's departmental store, but since leased to Alders. Facing the camera is part of Museum Terrace, a classically styled Victorian terrace fronting New London Road, also demolished in the 1960s to make way for the High Chelmer shopping precinct.

Since the 1960s the banks of the River Can have been concreted and public footpaths created on either side. The only feature remaining from the earlier picture is the New London Road bridge.

2

Around the Centre

Bishop's Court was a magnificent mansion built in 1890 by Walter Ridley of the brewing firm; it stood in 9 acres of land. The house was acquired by the Church of England when the Diocese of Chelmsford was created in 1914, but was demolished in the 1970s. Houses now stand here.

Moulsham Street, *c.* 1925. The photographer is looking towards the town centre, with the Grove Road turning immediately on the right, and the entrance to New Writtle Street further down on the left. As now, there was a variety of two-storey shops and pubs, giving the air of a village street.

Even today this part of Moulsham Street retains its cosy appearance. Few of the buildings have been replaced although uses have changed. One honourable exception is the chemist immediately on the right, which has been there for many a year.

Moulsham Street, c. 1905, looking towards London from near the present junction with The Parkway. The narrow road emphasises the fact that Moulsham was once a separate village.

Despite changes in the intervening years, much of the street's character still remains, with shops and houses huddled alongside each other. Sadly, though, some of the newer buildings are to designs not consistent with the traditional styles.

The upper part of Moulsham Street, looking towards High Street, *c.* 1905. The Victorian St John's church is on the right, within its well-kept graveyard, and the Church School is adjoining.

The school was converted into residential flats in the 1980s. Additional planting has taken place in the churchyard but otherwise, apart from the distant view of the Cater building, the scene is recognisable today.

Chelmsford Infirmary and Dispensary was opened in New London Road in 1883, surrounded by a neat garden. Initially it was merely a small cottage hospital, with limited accommodation, but with a quickly growing urban population, fuelled by a rapid expansion of local industries, it soon became an essential part of the community, with additional wards built at the rear.

In the latter part of the twentieth century local needs were met instead by Broomfield Hospital, and the rear extensions demolished. However, the original infirmary building has been adapted into a health centre. Sadly the ornamental brick boundary wall has long since been replaced by a more utilitarian fence.

Thornwood, a handsome detached house in New London Road, was built towards the end of the nineteenth century and later became a nurses' home for the adjacent hospital.

Following the closure of the hospital in the 1980s the property was sold, and renovated for use as offices.

At the turn of the twentieth century New London Road was still a quiet highway. With considerable foresight, the nineteenth-century developers created a wide thoroughfare well able to cope with traffic for over a century. Even today it manages moderately well, except at peak flow times.

The road remains an impressive entrance to the town, thanks to the continued existence of many classical-style houses, now mostly converted into offices.

Many large and well-designed villas and houses were built along New London Road. One of these was Bellfields, the back of which is seen here, together with part of its imposing garden. When this picture was taken, in 1913, it was the home of the first Mayor of Chelmsford, Cllr Frederick Chancellor JP. It was later used by the hospital as a convalescent home, presided over by a fiery Scottish nursing sister.

In the 1980s most of the land occupied by the hospital, including Bellfields, was redeveloped for offices. Sadly the attractive Victorian open balconies, which were such a feature of the rear of the building, have disappeared, and have been replaced by a low-maintenance structure, producing a much blander appearance.

New Street from under the Great Eastern Railway bridge, *c.* 1900. Wells & Perry Brewery and the Brewers House are on the left, with the Lion and Lamb pub in the distance. Immediately on the right is the Railway Tavern, then a pub with a dubious reputation. In the late 1920s Victoria Road was created from Duke Street to New Street, from next to the Brewers House. The latter was demolished in the 1970s to make way for the present office block.

Although the road and railway themselves remain the Railway Tavern, seen on the right, is the only building to survive from earlier times.

A quiet summer's day in Duke Street, *c.* 1910. An overhanging branch from one of the adjoining properties softens the scene.

On the northern side of the road many of the older buildings still remain, providing a foil for the Cathedral. On the southern side, however, to the right of the picture the massive 1930s neo-Georgian County Hall has replaced the earlier properties.

Chelmsford Library and Museum in Market Road, now Victoria Road South, was built by Frederick Chancellor in 1905 with the fledgeling Chelmsford School of Science and Art occupying the upper rooms. It was from here that the present Anglia Polytechnic University and the Chelmer Valley High School were to develop. A horse can be seen grazing on adjacent land.

Remarkably little change has taken place during the intervening years to this pleasant building, now renamed the Chancellor Building. It is still used for educational purposes, together with other land in the vicinity, as part of Anglia Polytechnic University. A Baptist church now occupies the adjoining site. The library and museum now have premises elsewhere.

The Territorial Army Association's building in Market Road, now Victoria Road South, seen here in 1980, was opened at the turn of the twentieth century and for many years was the home of the Essex Yeomanry. Prior to the Second World War there was a large drill hall adjoining, occupied by the Essex Regiment. It was destroyed during the war, when it received a direct hit by enemy aircraft.

The Association building was demolished in 1997 and the whole site is now occupied by a striking new office block, which in 1999 won an architectural award from the local amenity society.

The railway station, Duke Street, *c.* 1905, which remained virtually unchanged until about 1980, when major remodelling took place. On the forecourt the Saracen's Head's horse omnibus awaits hotel guests, whilst a Stratford-built Great Eastern Railway bus is also on hand for passengers.

The replacement station, built in the 1980s, is a somewhat disappointing structure, of even more modest appearance than the original. Although internally it has improved facilities, externally it somewhat resembles a large lean-to shed.

Passengers patiently await the arrival of the London-bound train at Chelmsford railway station, *c.* 1905.

Ninety-five years later the platforms are little changed. The main difference lies in the appearance of the passengers, who are now much less formally dressed.

Colchester-bound GER steam train approaches Chelmsford station, *c.* 1905.

Nearly a hundred years later the trains have totally changed, being driven by overhead electric power. However, a link with the past is preserved in the current trading name 'Great Eastern' for the suburban line trains.

Duke Street, 1929. On the left is the Eastern National bus station just prior to rebuilding, when the site was expanded towards Fairfield Road by incorporating the site of the large house seen beyond. Further reconstruction took place in 1938 when the site was further extended and the present station built. It was then hailed as one of the most modern in the country.

The bus station now runs from Viaduct Road in the foreground to Fairfield Road in the distance. It offers a frequent service to most parts of central Essex. Buildings facing it remain largely unchanged. However, the station and garage behind are now regarded as outmoded, and redevelopment is likely within the next few years.

Duke Street, looking towards the railway station on a day with sparse traffic, c. 1920.

The Civic Centre and the Eastern National bus station now occupy the land on the right-hand side, but few of the buildings on the left have been rebuilt, although they now have different uses. The slender spire of the Cathedral is seen above the railway bridge.

At the turn of the century Fairfield Road was a quiet and select Victorian cul-de-sac, with a well-known local builder living at the end of the road, next to his yard.

The properties were swept away in the 1930s to make way for an extension to the Eastern National bus station, on one side, and the former Borough Library on the other. The adjoining Civic Theatre (further from the camera) was built in post-war years. The builder's yard, together with additional land, is now a large municipal car park.

The Pavilion cinema opened in 1920. Internally its design followed that of a simple rectangular hall, with a tiny foyer and an elaborate façade in the then-fashionable Egyptian style. Until the appearance of 'talkies' it screened silent films. During the Second World War it suffered considerable bomb damage, which resulted in the façade being rebuilt in a plainer style.

Now converted into a nightclub, a large and rather grotesque image has been added to the façade, and several sad potted palms sit on the forecourt. Shops and offices have now replaced the adjoining gardens.

Viaduct Road, *c.* 1925. A National Bus Company Guy charabanc stands outside the railway arches near Duke Street, ready to take on passengers. The white-coated conductor stands proudly besides the seated driver.

Ever since the massive railway viaduct was built in the 1840s it has provided useful storage for various enterprises, including the first buses. Today the arches are being renovated, and when complete they will continue to provide accommodation for a variety of activities.

The Red Cow Temperance Hotel at the corner of Broomfield Road and Rainsford Road, *c.* 1905, was a very attractive detached property, with a well-kept front garden. The owner was a Mr Bausor. On his death the house was used as auction rooms and, even later, a branch of Barclays Bank.

After some years of abuse it has now been demolished and the future use of the site is in doubt. On the opposite side of the road the former houses are now offices, whilst the ungainly bulk of Britvic House can be seen in the distance.

Duke Street, looking towards the station, *c.* 1935. On the right is the neo-Georgian Public Library built in 1933. Opposite is a three-storey 1920s red-brick structure, with shops and flats over. The garden seen in the foreground belongs to Rainsford House, an Edwardian property which was used as Council offices at this time.

Today most of the buildings seen in the upper picture remain; nevertheless, the scene is much busier, with cars replacing the bicycles. The gardens in the foreground have given way to a paved concourse in front of the Civic Centre, which replaced Rainsford House in the 1960s.

The war memorial was erected in Duke Street in front of Rainsford House during the 1920s, commemorating all those Chelmsfordians killed on military service during the First World War. Behind is a glimpse of the ivy-covered wall of Rainsford House.

In the 1950s a further inscription was added to the monument, dedicated to all Chelmsfordians killed during the Second World War, thereby recognising that civilians, as well as soldiers, lost their lives as part of the war effort. The annual Remembrance Day service takes place next to it.

A view of Rainsford House whilst still in use as a private house, taken from the once-extensive gardens at the rear *c.* 1910.

The site, together with adjoining land, was redeveloped in stages throughout the 1960s as council offices, with ancillary car parking.

The junction of Rainsford Road and Rainsford Lane, *c.* 1905. Although the former was the main road to Sawbridgeworth and Bishops Stortford there was only light traffic. Rainsford Lane was connected to Waterhouse Lane by a flimsy bridge over the River Can.

Today this intersection is one of the busiest in the town, with London to Braintree traffic speeding across the crossing. In place of the pleasant gardens on the far side there is now a large motor car showroom, and the peaceful scene has gone for ever.

Until the latter part of the last century it was usual for livestock to be driven 'on the hoof' to Chelmsford's thriving market. Here, in 1910, a small herd passes St Peter's church hall, now demolished. On the left are Victorian terrace houses, whose most attractive features were the uniform sash windows and ornamental wrought-iron front garden fences.

Sadly the ironwork was removed during the war to make munitions, and the regular appearance of the terrace has been damaged by modern 'improvements', such as u-PVC windows, porches and rendering.

The Essex Industrial and Home School for Destitute Boys, commonly known as the Home School, opened in substantial grounds off Rainsford Road in 1872. The regime was spartan, but the boys were taught useful trades, including that of market gardening, providing their own vegetables from the surrounding land.

The school closed in the 1970s. Today the line of trees marking the entrance drive still survives, but the gardens were redeveloped for residential purposes in the late 1990s.

During the First World War the Compasses pub in Broomfield Road was a popular meeting place for many of the troops billeted in and around the town. Here, squaddies gather together with some of the locals for a group picture.

In the 1930s the pub was rebuilt on an enlarged site in the then-fashionable 'pub Tudor' style, and to this day remains a popular watering hole.

Tower Gardens in Admirals Park derives its name from a large municipal Victorian water tower (demolished in the 1960s) sited next to Rainsford Road. For over 100 years the gardens have included several well-patronised public hard and grass tennis courts. They are in constant use during the summer months as a Mecca for aspiring tennis players and keep-fit enthusiasts.

The increasing popularity of bowls has resulted in the grass courts pictured in the upper picture being converted into a bowling lawn, although both hard and soft courts remain.

King Edward VI Grammar School, seen here in about 1905, is commonly known as KEGS. It was originally in Duke Street, on land now occupied by County Hall, but transferred in 1890 to the present site in Broomfield Road. Over the years it has steadily expanded, with new buildings at the rear.

From the road the premises are little altered. The school is noted for its excellent academic record, and is one of a handful of state grammar schools surviving in Essex. Part of the land in the foreground has been lost to road improvements, bringing the main buildings closer to the road.

Coval Lodge is an attractive one- and two-storey Grade II listed property near Rainsford Road, and at the turn of the century it was surrounded by a large and attractive garden.

Sadly much of the former garden has been developed, but the house remains, though hemmed in by newer buildings. Nevertheless it remains an oasis of beauty and tranquillity within a heavily built-up area.

The three-storey turreted police station, built in 1907 at the junction of New Street and Waterloo Lane, was conveniently sited close to the Shire Hall, seen on the left. It continued in use as the local station until the 1960s, when a new building was built further down New Street. A tunnel ran from the station to the Shire Hall, through which prisoners could be escorted to the courts.

The building is now used as offices, and the former cells provide a novel venue for a nightclub.

Hoffmann's Works, New Street, *c*. 1925. At its peak, in the 1940s, some 5,000 people were employed at the factory, making industrial ball and roller bearings. It was the largest factory of its kind in the British Commonwealth and played a vital role in the Second World War. As a result of post-war amalgamations and foreign competition, the factory closed in 1989 and most of the buildings were demolished, including those in the foreground.

The surviving four-storey building has been converted into high-class flats, whilst the rest of the site is now occupied by the Anglia Polytechnic University, founded from the Chelmer Institute of Higher Education. Its main block, Queens Building, is just left of centre.

Chelmsford's first purpose-built swimming pool was opened in Waterloo Lane in 1906. Before this Chelmsfordians had made use of the Central Park Lake and local rivers. The new facility was an instant success, even though it was unheated and open only during the summer months. Water for the pool was taken directly from the adjacent River Chelmer after passing through sand filter beds. Slipper baths were also provided within the complex. In the early part of the last century these were well patronised, as few houses then had bathrooms.

A municipal car park now occupies most of the site, together with a small open-air swimming pool and promenade. A leisure centre, including a large indoor swimming pool, adjoins.

Springfield Road, at the junction of Navigation Road, *c.* 1915, was a beautiful tree-lined avenue flanked by attractive Victorian detached mansions.

Most of the old properties have now been demolished or converted into offices, and face a road with constant heavy traffic.

A quiet scene in Springfield Road, looking towards Sandford Road and Colchester, *c.* 1910. On the left are two-storey properties, some of which, even in those days, had been converted into shops. In the distance is the Endeavour pub. The ornate cast-iron front garden railings on the right were removed as part of the war effort in 1940, and sadly not replaced.

Today this road serves the outlying estates.

Chelmsford Gaol was built in Springfield Road in 1828, replacing the earlier one in Moulsham Street. The entrance, seen here, was constructed of Bramley Fall Stone to an Egyptian style. In the nineteenth century public executions for comparatively minor offences took place on the flat roof. During the First World War and for several years afterwards the prison was taken over by the War Department to accommodate prisoners of war and military prisoners.

In the 1970s the entrance was rebuilt to the present style, when major refurbishment of the gaol took place. A car park was created at the same time outside the entrance.

In earlier times Springfield village was a small community straddling the old Roman road towards Colchester, with its church and village green on a side road to Broomfield. On the right is the Plough pub, and the village smithy is on the left, with various cottages.

The Plough is still remarkably unchanged, and is well placed to serve the housing estates which have now engulfed the locality. The old smithy has become a petrol station and the cottages have gone.

This building, on the corner of Hall Street and Mildmay Road, was built in 1861 as a silk weaving factory, but in 1898 was taken over by Guglielmo Marconi, and became the first radio factory in the world. In 1912 it became a furniture repository when Marconi moved to purpose-built premises in New Street.

In the 1990s the structure was completely refurbished, and is now part of the head office of the French-owned Essex & Suffolk Water Company.

At the junction of the River Can and the Chelmer stands Moulsham Mill, *c.* 1905, a traditional timber-framed, weather-boarded structure, which goes back to medieval times. The waterwheels were able to use the combined flow of both rivers, although by the early part of the last century a steam roller plant had been installed. Flour was once taken from the mill via the adjacent waterway but in post-war years it was used only for the production of animal feed.

In the 1960s a major flood prevention scheme was carried out in Chelmsford which diverted the river away from the restored mill.

A rear view of Moulsham Mill, *c.* 1900, showing the sturdy brick Victorian addition which housed the steam roller plant. Initially coal to stoke the furnaces was brought by barge, but later it was carted in from the New Street railway goods yard. Nevertheless the waterwheel continued to be used from time to time.

The mill was derelict for some time after the water channel was moved, but was subsequently reopened and is occupied by a conference centre and individual start-up enterprises.

In the 1930s considerable residential development took place on the fringes of the town – a process which still continues. Most houses of that era were semi-detached, with comparatively large gardens. These properties, part of a group of sixteen similar houses in Sandford Road, were somewhat ahead of their time as they included integral garages. It was a matter of pride to keep the front gardens spick and span, with well-tended hedges and lawns.

Today the houses have a less 'homely' appearance as new frontages have been created and functional, weatherproof u-PVC windows fitted. The rise of the two- or even three-car family has in many cases meant sacrificing the leafy privacy of the front garden for the wide-open spaces of the garage forecourt; while the garage itself may have found other uses.

A new water main was laid in Vicarage Road in about 1950, causing a great deal of disturbance. The heavy steel pipes were craned individually into a carefully levelled trench, bolted together and then tested for leakage. Today the work is considerably easier, as it merely consists of laying a continuous blue plastic pipe into the waiting trench and replacing the surface.

Road works had long since been completed when this shot was taken in June 2000 and the street has become a quiet cul-de-sac. The double glazing salesman's art has lent a rather uniform aspect to the houses, and, as on the previous page, much green space has been given up to the needs of the motor car.

At the turn of the twentieth century a simple ford, together with a wooden footbridge over the River Can, linked Rainsford Road with Waterhouse Lane. A few years later the ford was replaced by a narrow lightweight bridge, which remained until post-war years.

The present concrete structure was built in the 1950s to take increasing traffic from Braintree and Dunmow to London.

The Sunbeam Café in Prince's Road, *c.* 1935. It was a well-known meeting place for motorists and cyclists seeking cheap refreshments, and was particularly popular with those travelling along the newly built bypass.

Over the years the premises have been progressively extended and altered, and are now known as the Miami Motel & Restaurant. Vehicle designs seem to have come full-circle!

Springfield Mill in Victoria Road was in continuous use as a flour mill for 200 years. It later produced animal feed and fertiliser.

After becoming a store in post-war years it was derelict for a time, but in the 1970s it was attractively converted into a public house and restaurant.

3

Waterways and Open Space

The Conduit, once sited in High Street, now provides an attractive feature in Tower Gardens, Rainsford Road.

Seen here in about 1938, the Memorial Gardens were a substantial area of open space and mature landscaping dedicated to Chelmsfordians killed in the Boer War. The River Can formed one boundary and the cattle market the other. When the High Chelmer shopping precinct was constructed, a substantial strip of the gardens was incorporated into the new development to provide for servicing and access, with the monument resited nearer the river.

Following the redevelopment the gardens were extended along the river bank to New London Road, and although reduced in width they are far more used today – and are popular in summer lunchtimes with office workers.

The Recreation Ground, now Central Park, was created by Chelmsford Council towards the end of
the nineteenth century. Shortly after they were able to lease – and later buy – the lake, actually a
flooded barrow pit dug by the Eastern Counties Railway Company to provide soil for the adjacent
railway embankment. The magnificent brick viaduct carrying the track over the River Can marked
the western end of the Park. In this picture a steam train is approaching the railway station from
London, *c.* 1930.

The same scene today, with an electric train nearing the station. The lake is now a popular venue
for local anglers, and well-marked fishing stations are provided along the fringes.

The well-shaded footpath running between the Central Park lake and the railway embankment has been a favourite spot for courting couples for generations.

It remains little changed today.

A riverside walk from New London Road (pictured here in about 1920) ran through Memorial Gardens into the Recreation Ground, now Central Park, and was a well-used walk for Chelmsfordians from the time the gardens opened. A rustic footbridge once crossed the river allowing people to stroll from New London Road on the south side of the river.

Following the construction of the High Chelmer shopping precinct, a new footpath was created on the north side of the river, providing a continuous route through the town centre on that side of the water.

The River Can, with Central Park on the left bank, *c.* 1950. The bridge provided foot access to Chelmsford City Football Club's grounds in New Writtle Street. The river was later widened and deepened as part of a channel improvement in the 1960s, but has since regained its natural appearance.

It is seen here during a rare summer flood, June 2000.

The River Can, looking upstream, with a glimpse of Memorial Gardens on the right-hand bank, 1950. The pathway led to the recreation ground.

Superficially the scene has little changed. Nevertheless, invisible behind the trees, the Parkway now crosses the river at this point and the continuous roar of traffic dominates this once-peaceful spot. On the opposite bank, wedged between the river and the Parkway, a new area of garden has been created. Remarkably the Scots pine seen in the upper picture still survives.

The River Can from New London Road Bridge, *c.* 1935. In those times a bridge carried a footpath diagonally over the river, providing access to the Memorial Gardens from the southern side of the road.

The 1960s flood prevention scheme resulted in the banks being concreted. At the same time the footbridge was removed, but in compensation a new footpath was created on the northern side. The builder's yard seen in the upper picture has been replaced by an office block.

The River Can downstream from New London Road Bridge, still with a rural appearance, *c.* 1900. The small windmill was used to pump water into a riverside garden.

The riverside is now thoroughly urbanised with departmental and lock-up shops both sides. Sadly, a rather plain bridge now partially masks the view of Moulsham Bridge, classified as an ancient monument and one of the more interesting features of the town.

In about 1900 the willow-lined River Chelmer wound upstream from Springfield Mill, creating an idyllic rural scene, with pastures on one side and a small dairy on the other.

The course of the river was changed in the 1960s and the bed infilled. It is now used as a car park for the so-called Egg Factory, seen on the right, which is built on the water meadows depicted in the picture above, thereby creating a real eyesore.

Springfield Basin, with two empty canal barges moored by Brown's warehouses at Coates Wharf, *c.* 1930. Contrary to the Chelmer Navigation Act of 1793 the public wharf at the head of the basin was being used for the storage of timber.

Within the last decade redevelopment has taken place around the basin, and attractively arranged flats have been built on part of Coates Wharf, with well-designed shops and flats on the former wharf area. A public concourse has been created around the head of the basin, providing for the first time foot access and public moorings for visiting pleasure craft.

Every year since 1797 the owners of the canal have carried out an inspection of the waterway. In pre-war days a borrowed horse-drawn working boat was cleaned out and converted into a committee room for the day. Here, Fred Hoy with Chelmsford Duke pulls the barge along Springfield Cut.

Susan, now owned by Chelmsford Museum Service, is the only surviving wooden barge on the canal, seen here in June 2000 on the same stretch of water. Walking alongside is Dr Geoff Bowles, Keeper of Science and Industry at Sandford Mill.

The massive flood prevention scheme under construction, *c.* 1960. In places completely new channels were excavated and elsewhere the existing course was widened and deepened, with the sides and bottom of the section passing through the town centre concreted. Stone Bridge was found to have no footings and these were inserted. The work was complicated by the need to maintain a flow at all times: therefore half of the channel was dealt with at a time.

This work proved to be the impetus for redevelopment, and although the Stone Bridge still remains the scene has totally changed. On the right is The Meadows shopping precinct, with the Cater building looming behind. On the left is the multi-screen Odeon cinema. New bridges criss-cross the river and a landscaped walkway provides riverside access.

Before the flood prevention scheme a small side channel existed, passing under the medieval Horsepond Bridge in Springfield Road before rejoining the main river. This picture, taken in about 1920, shows a rowing boat being navigated below the bridge from the horsepond.

A traffic roundabout now exists on this site, the watercourse having been completely infilled. Tesco now occupies the site of the slated- and pitched-roofed building on the left.

4

Nearby Villages

The triangular green at Writtle, seen here in about 1900, is one of the largest and most attractive village greens in Essex, and is surrounded by period houses of various ages. Although once a watering place for passing animals, Weir Pond at the Chelmsford end is now a home for ducks and geese.

Main Road, Boreham was a very rural spot at the turn of the twentieth century, and it was not uncommon for herds of livestock to be driven through here to Chelmsford market.

The Generals, an attractive listed medieval farmhouse, seen on the left, is now almost engulfed by urban sprawl spreading out from Boreham interchange.

Boreham House, built in 1728 and subsequently extended in 1822, is superbly sited at the far end of an artificial lake lined by ornamental trees. It was originally built as a private house for Benjamin Hoare, a wealthy banker.

It is now used for office purposes but externally it has changed little, although the massive trees pictured at the turn of the century were replaced by new planting in the 1950s.

The Griffin Hotel, situated near the top of Danbury Hill, has always been a welcome sight for the wayfarer, after enduring the long haul up from Sandon Brook. In 1905 the Great Eastern Railway Company started a feeder bus service between Danbury and Chelmsford railway station. This picture shows passengers seated in the open upper deck enjoying the extensive view, during a spell of fine weather.

Although buses still stop at the pub, its main trade is now mostly from passing motorists and local residents. Changes have been carried out to the fabric of the building, including the addition of window boxes and exposure of some of the gable timbers, replicating the appearance of a Surrey public house rather than one in the eastern counties.

Many acres of open common land on the southern slopes of Danbury Hill are owned by the National Trust, and fine views can be enjoyed from here. Among the attractions is the well-sited Cricketers pub, seen here in about 1905.

It remains a popular watering hole. Sadly the village shop has been converted into a private house, as in so many other villages in Essex and beyond.

Galleywood Road, Great Baddow, *c.* 1900. This was a tree-shaded lane leading out of the village and a popular place for a quiet stroll. St Mary the Virgin's tall leaded spire can just be seen above the trees.

It is now a well-used through route from Great Baddow towards London, and has acquired a suburban character.

Great Waltham village street swings pleasantly around the parish church of St Mary & St Lawrence, *c.* 1910, with cottages, shops and public houses close by. A milk float is seen proceeding along an otherwise deserted High Street, delivering the morning 'pinta'.

Although the road still winds through the village, many of the buildings pictured a century ago have gone. The Beehive, seen in the foreground, was rebuilt in the 1950s set back from the road junction.

High Street, Little Waltham, *c.* 1910. This is a pleasant village between Chelmsford and Braintree, containing many medieval buildings. At this time it was a similar size to its neighbour, Great Waltham.

Today the centre of the village remains unchanged, although cars have made their inevitable appearance in the scene. Suburban-style development has been built on the fringes, and the village today has a much larger population than its sister community.

New Hall is a large Tudor mansion standing in its own grounds at Boreham, just off the old main Chelmsford to Colchester road. It was surrounded by good-quality agricultural land, sadly now giving way to a rash of unremarkable modern housing. The long drive to New Hall from the Colchester Road was marked by twin gatehouses, built in the style of the mansion. In 1910 they stood in splendid isolation.

The attractive old structures have recently been demolished, and the site is now derelict.

c. 1950. Writtle Mill was located on the River Wid near the entrance to the village on the Chelmsford Road. It was an attractive two-storey red-brick structure, built in 1877 on the site of an earlier mill, and although intended for flour grinding for most of its life it was used for preparing animal feed. It became a store after 1957 when the river was diverted, and unfortunately was destroyed by fire in the 1980s.

The site is now derelict and a charming scene has completely disappeared. Only a tree which once guarded the entrance survives. Perhaps the land will be allowed to remain open, thereby retaining distant views of Widford Church.

In 1900 Broomfield was a quiet agricultural village astride the Chelmsford to Braintree road, with houses grouped around a small green. The Angel, seen on the right, was a popular stopping place for the thirsty traveller.

In the last fifty years the village has become virtually a suburb of Chelmsford, although it retains a certain leafy charm. Following the construction of the Essex Regiment Way, the Angel no longer serves the traveller, but provides a useful service to the local community.

St John's Road, Writtle, looking towards the River Wid and Chelmsford, edged on either side by small timber-framed cottages, *c.* 1905. In the distance is the Writtle Brewery.

Most of the old cottages have now been replaced by modern housing and a garage has superseded the old brewery.

In the 1920s a welcome sight for the traveller approaching Writtle from Chipping Ongar was this garage and café with its choice of different brands of petrol.

Although much changed, the garage remains, but the former café is now a car showroom.

Watchhouse Road, Galleywood, was still a rural area in the early 1950s, with cows being driven to and from the farm for milking. To the right is the Old Blue Lion, with a line of cycles leaning against the side wall – their owners no doubt enjoying a well-deserved pint.

The farm buildings have been replaced by modern development and the country lane has become just another suburban road – fortunately the pub survives.